# SECRET OF MANIFESTING DREAMS

## A WOMAN'S GUIDE TO INTENTIONAL LIVING

## DR. MINAKSHI BANSAL

# Contents

# Contents

# Contents

# Prayer

*"Om Bhadram Karnebhih Shrinuyama Devah*

*Bhadram Pashyemakshabhiryajatrah*

*Sthirairangais Tushtuvamsastanubhih*

*Vyashema Devahitam Yadayuh*

*Svasti Na Indro Vriddhashravah*

*Svasti Nah Pusha Vishwavedah*

*Svasti Nastarkshyo Arishtanemih*

*Svasti No Brihaspatir Dadhatu*

*Om Shantih Shantih Shantih"*

*This mantra is a prayer for universal well-being, invoking the blessings of various deities for protection, health, and happiness. It emphasizes the importance of experiencing the auspicious through all senses and living a life aligned with divine purpose. The repetition of "Shantih" at the end signifies a deep desire for peace in the individual, the environment, and the universe at large. This mantra is often recited as a prayer for peace, prosperity, and the physical and spiritual well-being of all beings.*

ᐁᐁᐁ

# About The Author

This book represents the culmination of extensive research and meticulous analysis, incorporating a diverse range of sources, including numerous books, scholarly studies, and personal experiences. Additionally, I have scoured various websites to gather relevant information and data essential for the compilation of this work. I have taken every precaution to ensure the accuracy of the information presented and have diligently cited all sources to acknowledge their contributions.

From her earliest days, Minakshi was distinguished by an insatiable appetite for reading. Her literary universe was inhabited by characters and narratives that spanned ethical tales, motivational and inspirational stories, and the mythic parables imbued with life lessons. This voracious reading habit was not merely for personal edification but was driven by a desire to distill and disseminate the essence of these narratives to foster the development of students and peers alike. She was particularly captivated by the lives and teachings of historical figures and spiritual leaders such as Adi Shankaracharya, Swami Vivekananda, Dr. APJ Abdul Kalam, Mahamana Pandit Madan Mohan Malviya, Mahatma Gandhi, Sardar Vallabhai Patel, and Vinoba Bhave, among others. Their philosophies and life stories fueled her ambition to embody their ideals of resilience, selflessness, and relentless pursuit of knowledge.

Dr. Minakshi's academic and practical engagement with psychology has been equally noteworthy. As a research scholar, her focus has been on exploring the intricate tapestry of the human psyche, aiming to unlock the potential for psychological well-being and societal harmony. Her scholarly work is complemented by her active involvement in social work, where she employs her academic insights to make tangible differences in the lives of the underprivileged. Her endeavours in social work are characterized by an innovative approach that combines traditional wisdom with contemporary psychological practices to address the multifaceted challenges faced by these communities.

Her artistic talents, another facet of her diverse capabilities, are not merely a personal passion but also serve as a medium through which she communicates and connects with others. Her art, rich in symbolism and emotional depth, reflects her philosophical inquiries and social concerns, offering viewers a glimpse into the breadth of her intellect and the depth of her compassion.

In addition to her contributions to the arts and social sciences, Dr. Minakshi has embraced the healing arts of Pranic Healing, mastering the techniques developed by Master Choa Kok Sui. This practice, which focuses on the manipulation of Prana or life energy to heal the body and aura, has been both a personal journey of discovery and a means through which she extends her healing touch to others. Her proficiency in Pranic Healing is complemented by her advocacy and teaching of various forms of meditation aimed at rejuvenation, personal betterment, and the cultivation of harmony within individuals and communities alike.

Dr. Minakshi's life is a narrative of relentless pursuit, not just of personal achievement but of the upliftment and empowerment of society at large. Her diverse interests and talents—spanning the arts, literature, psychology, and the healing practices—converge on a singular path of service. She embodies the spirit of the luminaries who inspired her, channelling their legacy through her actions and teachings. Through her books, art, and social initiatives, she continues to inspire a new generation to embark on their own journeys of self-discovery, resilience, and altruism.

Her commitment to social betterment, particularly her focus on uplifting underprivileged children, reflects a deep understanding of the transformative potential of education and personal development. By integrating her knowledge of psychology, her artistic sensibilities, and her healing practices, Dr. Bansal has developed a holistic approach to social work that addresses both the immediate needs and the long-term well-being of the communities she serves.

As an author, Dr. Minakshi's writings offer a blend of inspirational insights, practical wisdom, and reflective contemplations drawn from her extensive reading and life experiences. Her books serve as a guide for those seeking to navigate the complexities of life with grace, resilience, and purpose. Through her narratives, she extends an invitation to her readers to explore the depths of their own potential and to contribute meaningfully to the collective well-being of society.

In Dr. Minakshi Bansal, we find a remarkable synthesis of the artist, the scholar, the healer, and the social activist. Her life's work stands as a beacon of hope and a source of inspiration for individuals seeking to make a difference in the world. Her story is a compelling reminder of the power of individual action, rooted in compassion and driven by a profound commitment to the betterment of humanity. Dr. Minakshi's legacy is not just in the tangible outcomes of her efforts but in the enduring spirit of inquiry, empathy, and service that she embodies.

# Preface

In the tapestry of life, each woman carries within her an intricate weave of dreams, aspirations, and untapped potential. It is a tapestry that is both unique and universal, reflecting our individual experiences and the collective wisdom of women across time and cultures.

This book, my dear reader, is an invitation to explore this tapestry, to unravel its secrets, and to embark on a journey of intentional living, where you become the conscious creator of your own reality.

As a woman who has walked this path herself, I understand the challenges, the doubts, and the fears that can hold us back from fully embracing our dreams.

I have experienced firsthand the transformative power of intentionality, the magic that unfolds when we align our thoughts, feelings, and actions with our deepest desires. It is with this understanding and a deep passion for empowering women that I share with you the "Secrets of Manifesting Dreams."

This book is not a magic formula or a quick fix for achieving your goals. It is a guide, a roadmap, a companion on your journey of self-discovery and personal transformation. It is a collection of tools, techniques, and insights that I have gathered over the years through my own experiences, my studies, and my interactions with countless inspiring women.

The principles shared in this book are not new. They have been passed down through generations, whispered in sacred circles, and woven into the fabric of ancient wisdom traditions.

However, in our modern world, where we are bombarded with

distractions and external expectations, it is easy to lose sight of these timeless truths. This book serves as a gentle reminder, a beacon of light that illuminates the path back to our own inner wisdom and power.

The journey of manifesting dreams begins with awakening our inner visionary, uncovering our deepest desires, and creating a compelling vision for our lives.

It involves harnessing the power of intention, cultivating gratitude, releasing limiting beliefs, and designing a life that is aligned with our values, passions, and purpose. It is a journey that requires courage, perseverance, and a willingness to step outside of our comfort zones.

This book is not just about achieving external goals; it is about transforming our inner world. It is about cultivating a positive mindset, embracing our imperfections, and developing a deep sense of self-love and acceptance. It is about finding our flow, connecting with our intuition, and embracing change as an opportunity for growth. It is about creating a sacred space for self-care and nurturing our mind, body, and spirit.

It is my hope that this book will serve as a guide and a source of inspiration for women everywhere who are seeking to live a more intentional and fulfilling life.

May it empower you to embrace your dreams, to tap into your infinite potential, and to create a life that is a true reflection of your authentic self.

Remember, the journey of manifesting dreams is not a solo endeavor. We are all interconnected, and we rise together. Surround yourself with a supportive community of like-minded women who will uplift and inspire you. Share your dreams, your challenges, and your triumphs with them.

Together, we can create a world where every woman feels empowered to manifest her dreams and live a life of joy, abundance, and fulfillment.

May this book be a catalyst for your own personal transformation, a stepping stone on your journey towards manifesting your dreams. May it empower you to step into your full potential, to embrace your authentic self, and to create a life that is a true reflection of your heart's desires.

***Dr. Minakshi Bansal***
***Social Activist***
***Ahmedabad, Gujarat, Bharat***

# ONE

# Awakening Your Inner Visionary: Uncover your deepest desires and create a compelling vision for your life.

Every woman carries within her an untapped reservoir of dreams and aspirations, a wellspring of potential waiting to be unleashed. Awakening your inner visionary is a journey of self-discovery, a process of peeling back the layers of societal conditioning and expectations to uncover your authentic desires and create a compelling vision for your life.

It begins with self-reflection, a deep dive into the depths of your being. Take the time to explore your passions, values, and beliefs. What ignites your soul? What makes your heart sing? What do you truly value in life? What are your core beliefs about yourself and the world around you? These questions may seem simple, but the answers hold the key to unlocking your inner visionary.

As you delve deeper into self-reflection, you'll start to notice patterns and themes emerging. These are the clues that lead you to your deepest desires, the dreams that have been lying dormant within you. It's important to be honest with yourself, to let go of any fears or doubts that may be holding you back. Remember, this is your journey, and you are the only one who can truly define what you want out of life.

Once you've identified your deepest desires, it's time to create a compelling vision for your life. This is where your inner visionary truly comes to life. Your vision is your North Star, guiding you towards your dreams and aspirations. It's a picture of your ideal life, a vivid representation of what you want to achieve and experience.

To create your vision, start by setting aside some time for quiet contemplation. Find a peaceful space where you can relax and let your mind wander. Close your eyes and imagine yourself living your dream life. What does it look like? What does it feel like? Who are you with? What are you doing?

As you visualize your ideal life, allow yourself to feel the emotions that come up. Excitement, joy, peace, fulfillment – these are the emotions that will fuel your motivation and drive you towards your goals. Write down your vision in detail, using words that resonate with you and evoke powerful emotions.

Your vision is a living, breathing entity that will evolve and grow with you. It's not set in stone, but rather a dynamic roadmap that guides you on your journey. As you move closer to your dreams, your vision may shift and change, and that's okay. Embrace the evolution and allow your vision to inspire and motivate you along the way.

Awakening your inner visionary is a lifelong journey of self-discovery and growth. It's about uncovering your authentic desires, creating a compelling vision for your life, and taking inspired action towards your dreams. Remember, you are the author of your own story, and you have the power to manifest the life you desire. So, embrace your inner visionary and let your dreams take flight.

ೲೲೲ

*Your dreams are a sacred map to your soul's purpose. Uncover your deepest desires, and let your intention be the compass that guides you towards their realization. Remember, your dreams are not just for you; they are a gift to the world.*

# TWO

# THE POWER OF INTENTION: HARNESS THE ENERGY OF FOCUSED INTENTION TO MANIFEST YOUR DREAMS INTO REALITY.

Intention, often underestimated, is a potent force that shapes our lives. It is the driving energy behind our actions, decisions, and ultimately, our manifestations. It is the compass that guides us towards our desired outcomes and the fuel that propels us forward.

When harnessed consciously, intention becomes a powerful tool for manifesting dreams into reality.

At its core, intention is a focused form of energy. It is a clear, unwavering desire backed by a firm resolve to bring it into existence. It is not merely wishful thinking but a deliberate act of setting a course and committing to it. When we set an intention, we align our thoughts, feelings, and actions towards a specific goal. We create a magnetic field that attracts the resources, opportunities, and people necessary to manifest our dreams.

The power of intention lies in its ability to bridge the gap between the mental and the physical realms. Our thoughts are not just fleeting ideas; they are energy patterns that interact with the universe. When we focus our thoughts on a specific outcome, we send out a signal to the universe, which responds by aligning circumstances and events to match our desires.

However, harnessing the energy of intention requires more than just setting a goal and hoping for the best. It requires a focused and disciplined approach. The first step is to clarify your intention. What is it that you truly desire? What is the essence of your dream? Be specific, clear, and concise. The more precise your intention, the more powerful its manifestation will be.

Once you have clarified your intention, it's time to cultivate a strong belief in its possibility. Doubt and skepticism are like weeds that choke the seeds of your dreams. Nurture a positive mindset, trust in the process, and believe that your intention will manifest. This unwavering faith creates a fertile ground for your dreams to take root and flourish.

Another crucial aspect of harnessing the power of intention is taking aligned action. Intention without action is like a car without fuel; it won't get you very far. Once you have set your intention, take steps that move you closer to your goal. This could involve learning new skills, seeking out opportunities, or simply showing up consistently and doing the work.

As you take aligned action, it's important to remain open and receptive to the signs and synchronicities that the universe presents. These are often subtle nudges in the right direction, confirmations that you are on the right path. Pay attention to your intuition, follow your gut instincts, and trust that the universe is conspiring to help you achieve your dreams.

Maintaining a positive attitude and gratitude for the blessings in your life is also crucial for harnessing the power of intention. A grateful heart attracts abundance and opens the door to even greater manifestations. Celebrate your successes, no matter how small, and express gratitude for the lessons learned along the way.

Harnessing the energy of focused intention is a transformative process that empowers you to create the life you desire. It is a journey of self-discovery, growth, and manifestation. By clarifying your intentions, cultivating a strong belief, taking aligned action, remaining open and receptive, maintaining a positive attitude, and expressing gratitude, you can tap into the limitless potential of the universe and manifest your dreams into reality. Remember, your intention is your most powerful tool. Use it wisely, and watch as your dreams unfold before your very eyes.

ॐॐॐ

*Gratitude is the key that unlocks the door to abundance. When you focus on the blessings in your life, you open yourself up to receive even more. Let your heart overflow with gratitude, and watch as your life transforms into a masterpiece of abundance.*

# THREE

# Cultivating Gratitude: Embrace a grateful mindset and open yourself up to abundance.

Gratitude, often dismissed as a mere social pleasantry, is a potent force that holds the key to unlocking abundance in every aspect of life. It is not simply about saying "thank you" but an intentional shift in mindset that transforms our perception of the world and our place in it. By embracing gratitude, we open ourselves to a deeper appreciation of life's gifts, cultivating a sense of fulfillment and joy that transcends material possessions.

At its core, gratitude is a recognition of the good in our lives. It is a conscious acknowledgment of the blessings, both big and small, that we often take for granted. It is the act of pausing to appreciate the beauty of a sunrise, the warmth of a smile, or the support of a loved one. It is a shift in focus from what we lack to what we have, from what is wrong to what is right.

The practice of gratitude is a powerful antidote to negativity and discontent. It rewires our brains to focus on the positive, fostering a sense of optimism and resilience. When we actively seek out and appreciate the good in our lives, we train our minds to notice and savor those moments, creating a positive feedback loop that reinforces our gratitude.

Gratitude is not just a feeling; it is a way of being. It is a choice we make every day to focus on the abundance that surrounds us. It is a decision to see the glass half full, to find the silver lining in every cloud, and to appreciate the lessons learned from challenges. This shift in perspective opens the door to a wealth of possibilities, allowing us to see and seize opportunities that we might otherwise miss.

One of the most profound benefits of gratitude is its ability to attract abundance. When we express gratitude for what we have, we create a sense of receptivity that allows us to receive even more. Gratitude opens the floodgates to a flow of blessings, whether it's in the form of new relationships, career opportunities, or unexpected gifts. By focusing on the good, we create a magnetic field that draws more of it into our lives.

The practice of gratitude also has a profound impact on our well-being. It has been linked to improved physical health, increased happiness, reduced stress, and stronger relationships. When we feel grateful, our bodies release dopamine and serotonin, neurotransmitters that promote feelings of happiness and well-being. Gratitude also strengthens our immune system, lowers blood pressure, and improves sleep quality.

Cultivating gratitude is a journey, not a destination. It requires daily practice and commitment. There are many ways to cultivate gratitude, from keeping a gratitude journal to expressing appreciation for others. The key is to find practices that resonate with you and incorporate them into your daily routine.

Start by setting aside a few minutes each day to reflect on the things you are grateful for. Write them down in a journal, share them with a loved one, or simply contemplate them in silence. As you practice gratitude, you will begin to notice a shift in your perspective. You will find yourself focusing on the positive, appreciating the present moment, and feeling more connected to yourself and others.

As your gratitude grows, so will your abundance. You will attract more positive experiences, opportunities, and relationships into your life. You will feel more fulfilled, joyful, and at peace. You will discover that gratitude is not just a feeling but a way of life, a path to a richer, more meaningful existence.

In a world that often focuses on lack and negativity, cultivating gratitude is a radical act of self-love. It is a declaration that we are enough, that we have enough, and that we are worthy of abundance. By embracing gratitude, we open ourselves up to the limitless possibilities that life has to offer, creating a ripple effect of positivity that touches not only our own lives but also the lives of those around us.

❦❦❦

*Your thoughts are the architects of your reality. Challenge your limiting beliefs, and replace them with empowering affirmations that resonate with your soul. Remember, you are worthy, capable, and deserving of all that you desire.*

# FOUR

# Releasing Limiting Beliefs: Identify and overcome self-doubt and negative thought patterns.

Within each of us lies a boundless potential waiting to be unleashed, yet often we find ourselves held back by invisible chains—limiting beliefs. These are the deeply ingrained thoughts and assumptions about ourselves and the world that restrict our growth, hinder our progress, and dim our light. They are the voices of self-doubt that whisper "you're not good enough," "you can't do it," or "you don't deserve it." Recognizing and releasing these limiting beliefs is a transformative journey of self-discovery, empowerment, and liberation.

The first step in this journey is awareness. We must become conscious of the negative thought patterns that run on autopilot in our minds. These are the stories we tell ourselves about who we are, what we are capable of, and what is possible for us. They are often based on past experiences, societal conditioning, or the expectations of others. By paying attention to our thoughts and feelings, we can begin to identify the limiting beliefs that are holding us back.

Once we have identified our limiting beliefs, it's time to challenge their validity. Are they based on facts or fears? Are they serving us or sabotaging us? By questioning their truthfulness, we can begin to dismantle their power over us. We can replace them with empowering beliefs that support our growth and well-being.

One powerful way to challenge limiting beliefs is through affirmations. Affirmations are positive statements that we repeat to ourselves to reprogram our subconscious mind. By consciously choosing to focus on empowering thoughts, we can gradually shift our mindset and create new neural pathways that support our desired outcomes.

Another effective tool for releasing limiting beliefs is visualization. Visualization is the act of creating a mental picture of our desired reality. By vividly imagining ourselves achieving our goals and overcoming our challenges, we send a powerful message to our subconscious mind that these outcomes are possible. This, in turn, strengthens our belief in ourselves and our abilities.

Action is also essential in overcoming limiting beliefs. When we step outside of our comfort zones and take risks, we prove to ourselves that we are capable of more than we thought. We break down the walls of self-doubt and expand our horizons. Each small step we take towards our goals reinforces our belief in ourselves and our potential.

Seeking support from others can also be invaluable in this process. Surround yourself with positive, supportive people who believe in you and your dreams. Talk to a therapist or coach who can help you identify and address your limiting beliefs. Join a support group or online community where you can connect with others who are on a similar journey.

Remember, releasing limiting beliefs is not a one-time event; it is an ongoing process. It requires patience, perseverance, and self-compassion. There will be setbacks and challenges along the way, but don't give up. Keep moving forward, one step at a time, and celebrate your successes along the way.

By identifying and overcoming self-doubt and negative thought patterns, you open yourself up to a world of possibilities. You free yourself from the shackles of fear and self-imposed limitations. You step into your power and embrace your full potential. You become the architect of your own destiny, creating a life that is aligned with your deepest desires and aspirations.

ppp

*Your dream life is not a distant fantasy but a tangible reality waiting to be created. Design a roadmap for your ideal life, aligning your actions with your goals. Remember, every step you take towards your dreams is a victory worth celebrating.*

# FIVE

# DESIGNING YOUR DREAM LIFE: CRAFT A ROADMAP FOR YOUR IDEAL LIFE, ALIGNING YOUR ACTIONS WITH YOUR GOALS.

Designing your dream life is a transformative journey of self-discovery, intentionality, and action. It's a process of envisioning the life you truly desire and taking deliberate steps to create it. It's a roadmap to your ideal future, a blueprint for happiness, fulfillment, and success.

At the heart of this journey lies the power of intention. It's about identifying what truly matters to you, what makes your heart sing, and what brings you a sense of purpose and fulfillment. This deep introspection requires you to peel back the layers of societal expectations and societal conditioning to uncover your authentic desires and values. It's about discovering your passions, your strengths, and your unique gifts.

Once you've gained clarity on your deepest desires, it's time to craft a compelling vision for your dream life. This vision is your North Star, guiding you towards your goals and aspirations. It's a vivid picture of your ideal life, a tangible representation of what you want to create.

It encompasses all aspects of your life, from your career and relationships to your health, finances, and personal growth.

Your vision should be so clear and compelling that it excites and motivates you to take action. It should be a source of inspiration, a reminder of what's possible when you dare to dream big.

Write it down, create a vision board, or use any other tool that helps you visualize your dream life in detail. The more vivid your vision, the more powerful it will be in attracting your desired outcomes.

With your vision in place, it's time to start crafting a roadmap for your ideal life. This roadmap is your strategic plan for achieving your goals and making your vision a reality. It involves breaking down your big dreams into smaller, actionable steps, creating a timeline, and identifying the resources and support you'll need along the way.

Your roadmap should be specific, measurable, achievable, relevant, and time-bound (SMART). This means setting clear goals, defining the actions you'll take to achieve them, and establishing deadlines for completion. This approach ensures that you stay focused, motivated, and on track to create the life you desire.

Aligning your actions with your goals is a crucial aspect of designing your dream life. It's about making choices that support your vision and moving away from anything that doesn't serve it. It requires discipline, commitment, and a willingness to step outside of your comfort zone.

It's about saying "yes" to opportunities that align with your goals and "no" to distractions that pull you away from them.

This alignment also involves developing habits and routines that support your goals. It's about prioritizing self-care, investing in your personal growth, and surrounding yourself with positive, supportive people. It's about creating an environment that nurtures your dreams and empowers you to take action.

Remember, designing your dream life is not a destination, but a journey. It's a continuous process of growth, evolution, and refinement. Your vision and goals may change over time, and that's okay. The most important thing is to remain flexible, adaptable, and open to new possibilities.

Embrace the challenges and setbacks as opportunities for learning and growth. Celebrate your successes, no matter how small, and use them as fuel to propel you forward. Trust in the process, believe in yourself, and never lose sight of your dreams.

As you embark on this journey, remember that you are the architect of your own life. You have the power to create the life you desire.

By designing your dream life and aligning your actions with your goals, you can unlock your full potential and live a life that is truly extraordinary.

Designing your dream life is a transformative journey of self-discovery, intentionality, and action. It is about envisioning the life you truly desire and taking deliberate steps to create it. It is a roadmap to your ideal future, a blueprint for happiness, fulfillment, and success.

The first step in designing your dream life is to gain clarity on what you truly want. This involves exploring your passions, values, and aspirations. What makes your heart sing? What are you most passionate about? What are your core values?

What do you want to achieve in life? Take the time to reflect on these questions and write down your answers. The more specific and detailed you can be, the better.

Once you have a clear understanding of your desires, it's time to create a vision for your dream life. This is a visual representation of your ideal future, a picture of what you want to create. It can be a collage, a vision board, or simply a written description. The most important thing is that it resonates with you and inspires you to take action.

Your vision should encompass all aspects of your life, including your career, relationships, health, finances, and personal growth. Imagine yourself living your dream life in vivid detail. What does it look like? What does it feel like? Who are you with? What are you doing?

As you create your vision, allow yourself to dream big. Don't let fear or self-doubt hold you back. Remember, this is your dream life, and you have the power to create it. The more you believe in your vision, the more likely it is to become a reality.

Once you have a clear vision, it's time to start crafting a roadmap for your ideal life. This involves breaking down your big dreams into smaller, more manageable goals. What steps do you need to take to achieve your vision? What actions can you take today to move you closer to your goals?

Your roadmap should be specific, measurable, achievable, relevant, and time-bound (SMART). For example, instead of setting a vague goal like "I want to be successful," set a SMART goal like "I will increase my income by 10% in the next six months by taking on additional freelance projects and networking with potential clients."

As you create your roadmap, it's important to align your actions with your goals. This means making choices that support your vision and moving away from anything that doesn't. It may require making some sacrifices or changes in your life, but remember, the rewards will be worth it.

Designing your dream life is not a one-time event; it is an ongoing process. Your vision and goals may evolve over time, and that's okay. The most important thing is to stay committed to your journey and take consistent action towards your dreams.

Remember, you are the architect of your own life. You have the power to create the life you desire. By designing your dream life and taking aligned action, you can unlock your full potential and live a life that is truly fulfilling.

Here are some additional tips for designing your dream life:

Surround yourself with positive, supportive people who believe in you and your dreams.

Make time for self-care and prioritize your well-being.

Learn from your mistakes and setbacks, and use them as opportunities for growth.

Celebrate your successes along the way, no matter how small they may seem.

Be grateful for the blessings in your life and cultivate a positive mindset.

Remember, anything is possible if you believe in yourself and take action towards your dreams.

❧❧❧

*Self-care is not a luxury but a necessity. Nurture your mind, body, and spirit with love and compassion. Remember, you are a sacred vessel, and your well-being is essential for manifesting your dreams.*

# SIX

# THE ART OF SELF-CARE: NURTURE YOUR MIND, BODY, AND SPIRIT FOR OPTIMAL WELL-BEING AND CREATIVITY.

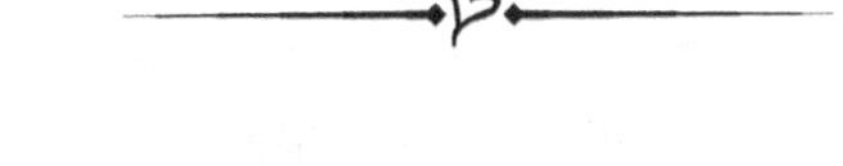

The art of self-care is a transformative practice that encompasses the nurturing of our mind, body, and spirit. It is not a luxury but a necessity, a fundamental pillar for optimal well-being and creativity. In the hustle and bustle of modern life, it's easy to neglect our own needs, prioritizing external demands over our inner well-being. However, true fulfillment and sustainable success arise from a place of balance and self-love. By embracing the art of self-care, we unlock our full potential and create a life that is both joyful and meaningful.

Nurturing the mind involves prioritizing mental and emotional well-being. It is about creating space for reflection, stillness, and inner peace. Engaging in activities that stimulate our intellect, such as reading, learning new skills, or engaging in thought-provoking conversations, keeps our minds sharp and agile. Cultivating a positive mindset through practices like mindfulness, meditation, and gratitude helps us manage stress, overcome challenges, and foster a sense of inner peace. It is equally important to set healthy boundaries, saying no to things that drain our energy and yes to those that nourish our souls.

The body, our physical vessel, requires care and attention to thrive. Regular exercise is essential for maintaining physical health, boosting energy levels, and promoting a positive mood. A balanced diet rich in nutrients provides the fuel we need to function optimally. Adequate sleep is crucial for rest and repair, allowing our bodies to recharge and rejuvenate. Equally important is taking time for relaxation and pleasure, whether it's indulging in a warm bath, getting a massage, or simply spending time in nature.

Nurturing our spirit involves connecting with our inner selves, our values, and our purpose. It is about finding meaning and fulfillment in our lives, exploring our creativity, and expressing our authentic selves. Engaging in spiritual practices such as meditation, prayer, or spending time in nature can help us connect with a higher power and find peace and tranquility. Pursuing our passions, whether it's art, music, writing, or any other creative endeavor, allows us to tap into our innate creativity and express our unique gifts.

The art of self-care is not a one-size-fits-all approach. It is a deeply personal journey that requires self-awareness and experimentation. What works for one person may not work for another. The key is to find practices that resonate with you and that you can incorporate into your daily life.

It is also important to remember that self-care is not selfish. By taking care of ourselves, we are better equipped to show up for others, to be more present, compassionate, and loving. When we are well-rested, nourished, and fulfilled, we have more to give to the world.

Incorporating self-care into our daily lives can have a profound impact on our well-being and creativity. It helps us reduce stress, improve our mood, boost our energy levels, and enhance our overall health. It also fosters creativity, allowing us to think more clearly, solve problems more effectively, and come up with innovative solutions.

By making self-care a priority, we create a ripple effect of positivity that touches every aspect of our lives. We become happier, healthier, more productive, and more fulfilled. We create a life that is aligned with our values, passions, and purpose. We become the best versions of ourselves, radiating love, light, and joy into the world.

ᐅᐅᐅ

*Your imperfections are not flaws but unique brushstrokes that add depth and beauty to your life's canvas. Embrace your vulnerabilities, and celebrate your journey of growth. Remember, you are perfectly imperfect, just as you are meant to be.*

# SEVEN

# EMBRACING IMPERFECTION: ACCEPT YOUR FLAWS AND CELEBRATE YOUR UNIQUE JOURNEY OF GROWTH.

In a world that often glorifies perfection, embracing imperfection can be a radical act of self-love and acceptance. It is a recognition that flaws are not blemishes on our character but rather integral parts of our unique human experience. Embracing imperfection is a journey of self-discovery, a process of learning to love and accept ourselves fully, with all our quirks, imperfections, and vulnerabilities.

It begins with a shift in perspective. Instead of viewing

imperfections as shortcomings, we can learn to see them as opportunities for growth and self-improvement. Every mistake, every setback, every perceived flaw is a chance to learn, to evolve, and to become a better version of ourselves. By embracing our imperfections, we open ourselves up to a world of possibilities, a path of continuous learning and growth.

Accepting our flaws does not mean resigning ourselves to mediocrity. It means recognizing that we are human, and that being human means being imperfect. It means acknowledging that we all have strengths and weaknesses, and that our imperfections do not define us. In fact, they often make us more relatable, more authentic, and more beautiful.

Embracing imperfection is also about celebrating our unique journey of growth. We are all on a lifelong journey of self-discovery, and our imperfections are a testament to the challenges we have faced and overcome. They are the scars that remind us of our resilience, our strength, and our capacity for growth. By celebrating our imperfections, we honor our journey and acknowledge the wisdom we have gained along the way.

It is important to remember that perfection is an illusion. It is a societal construct that sets unrealistic expectations and puts undue pressure on us to conform. By letting go of the pursuit of perfection, we free ourselves from the burden of comparison and self-criticism. We create space for self-acceptance, self-compassion, and self-love.

Embracing imperfection also allows us to cultivate a deeper sense of authenticity. When we accept our flaws, we are no longer hiding behind a mask of perfection. We are able to show up as our true selves, with all our quirks, imperfections, and vulnerabilities. This authenticity allows us to connect with others on a deeper level, to build meaningful relationships based on trust and acceptance.

Furthermore, embracing imperfection fosters a sense of resilience. When we accept that mistakes and setbacks are a natural part of life, we are less likely to be discouraged by them. We are able to bounce back from challenges with greater ease and grace, knowing that our imperfections do not define our worth or potential.

Embracing imperfection is a journey of self-discovery, self-acceptance, and self-love. It is a process of letting go of unrealistic expectations and embracing our humanity. It is a celebration of our unique journey of growth, a recognition that our imperfections are what make us beautiful, authentic, and resilient. By embracing imperfection, we open ourselves up to a life of greater joy, fulfillment, and connection.

*Your words have the power to shape your reality. Speak positive affirmations over your life, and watch as they transform your subconscious mind and attract your desires. Remember, your words are seeds that can blossom into a garden of abundance.*

# EIGHT

# The Power of Affirmations: Use positive affirmations to reprogram your subconscious mind.

Words possess a remarkable power to shape our reality. They have the ability to uplift, inspire, and motivate, or conversely, to tear down, discourage, and limit. Positive affirmations harness this power, utilizing carefully crafted statements to reprogram our subconscious mind and unlock our full potential. By consciously choosing to focus on empowering words and phrases, we can cultivate a positive mindset, overcome self-limiting beliefs, and manifest our desires into reality.

At their core, positive affirmations are declarations of truth, spoken or written in the present tense. They are not mere wishful thinking but rather statements of intention and belief. By repeating affirmations regularly, we begin to internalize them, gradually shifting our thoughts, feelings, and actions towards a more positive direction. The subconscious mind, which plays a crucial role in shaping our reality, is particularly receptive to affirmations. It absorbs the repeated messages, integrating them into our belief system and influencing our behavior.

The power of affirmations lies in their ability to bypass our conscious mind and directly access our subconscious. Our conscious mind is often filled with doubts, fears, and limiting beliefs that hold us back from achieving our goals. Positive affirmations, however, are designed to circumvent these mental blocks, creating new neural pathways that support our desired outcomes. They act as seeds planted in the fertile soil of our subconscious, gradually growing and blossoming into a more positive and empowering reality.

Choosing the right affirmations is crucial for their effectiveness. They should be specific, personal, and aligned with our goals and values. Generic affirmations may not resonate as deeply as those that are tailored to our individual needs and aspirations. It is also important to choose affirmations that are positive and empowering, avoiding negative language or self-deprecating statements.

Repetition is key to the success of affirmations. The more we repeat them, the more deeply they become ingrained in our subconscious mind. It is recommended to repeat affirmations several times a day, either aloud or silently, focusing on the meaning of the words and allowing ourselves to feel the emotions they evoke. Writing down affirmations and placing them in visible locations can also serve as a constant reminder of our positive intentions.

Affirmations are not a magic bullet, but rather a tool for personal transformation. They require consistent practice and a willingness to believe in their power. The effects may not be immediately apparent, but over time, you will begin to notice subtle shifts in your thoughts, feelings, and actions. You may find yourself becoming more confident, optimistic, and resilient. You may start to attract new opportunities and experience positive changes in your relationships and career.

In addition to their psychological benefits, affirmations have also been shown to have physiological effects. Studies have found that repeating positive affirmations can lower stress levels, boost the immune system, and even improve physical performance. This is because our thoughts and emotions have a direct impact on our physical well-being. By cultivating a positive mindset through affirmations, we create a ripple effect that extends to every aspect of our lives.

The power of affirmations lies not only in the words themselves but also in the intention and belief behind them. When we repeat affirmations with conviction and emotion, we send a powerful message to the universe that we are ready to manifest our desires. This unwavering faith creates a magnetic field that attracts the resources, opportunities, and people necessary to bring our dreams to life.

ppp

*Your tribe is your lifeline. Surround yourself with like-minded individuals who uplift and inspire you. Remember, you are not alone on this journey. Together, we rise.*

# NINE

# BUILDING A SUPPORTIVE COMMUNITY: SURROUND YOURSELF WITH LIKE-MINDED INDIVIDUALS WHO UPLIFT AND INSPIRE YOU.

The journey of life is enriched and empowered when we are surrounded by a supportive community. The bonds we form with like-minded individuals who uplift and inspire us are not merely social connections; they are the lifelines that sustain us through challenges, celebrate our victories, and propel us towards our highest potential. Building a supportive community is an intentional act of choosing the company we keep, cultivating relationships that nourish our souls, and fostering an environment where we can thrive.

The importance of community cannot be overstated. Humans are inherently social creatures, wired for connection and belonging. Throughout history, communities have provided a sense of safety, support, and shared purpose. They have been the cradles of culture, innovation, and collective growth.

In the modern world, where isolation and loneliness are becoming increasingly prevalent, the need for community is more pressing than ever.

Surrounding ourselves with like-minded individuals is not about conformity but about finding our tribe, people who share our values, passions, and aspirations. It is about connecting with those who understand our struggles, celebrate our successes, and challenge us to grow. When we are surrounded by people who believe in us and our dreams, we are more likely to believe in ourselves.

Their encouragement and support fuel our motivation, their wisdom and insights guide our path, and their presence reminds us that we are not alone.

Like-minded individuals can be found in a variety of settings, both online and offline. Joining clubs, groups, or organizations that align with our interests is a great way to meet people who share our passions. Attending workshops, conferences, or retreats can also provide opportunities to connect with like-minded individuals from all walks of life.

The internet has opened up a world of possibilities for building community, with countless online forums, groups, and social media platforms dedicated to specific interests and causes.

Building a supportive community is not just about finding like-minded individuals; it's also about cultivating meaningful relationships. This involves investing time and energy in getting to know people on a deeper level, sharing our thoughts and feelings, and offering support and encouragement in return. It's about creating a safe space where we can be ourselves, without fear of judgment or rejection.

Nurturing these relationships requires open communication, mutual respect, and a willingness to be vulnerable. It's about being present for each other, celebrating each other's successes, and offering a shoulder to lean on during challenging times. It's about building trust, loyalty, and a sense of belonging.

A supportive community is not only a source of emotional support; it can also be a catalyst for personal and professional growth. By surrounding ourselves with people who are passionate, motivated, and successful, we are inspired to raise our own standards and strive for greater heights.

We are challenged to think outside the box, to step out of our comfort zones, and to pursue our dreams with greater courage and determination.

Furthermore, a supportive community can provide us with valuable resources and opportunities. We can learn from each other's experiences, share knowledge and skills, and collaborate on projects that benefit the entire community. We can leverage each other's networks and connections to open doors and create new possibilities.

Building a supportive community is an investment in our own well-being and happiness. It is a choice we make to surround ourselves with people who uplift and inspire us, who challenge us to grow, and who support us on our journey. By cultivating meaningful relationships and fostering an environment of trust, respect, and mutual support, we create a powerful force for positive change in our lives and in the world.

❦❦❦

*Your passions are your compass. Follow your heart's desires, and engage in activities that bring you joy and fulfillment. Remember, your passions are not just hobbies; they are the keys to unlocking your true potential.*

# TEN

# FINDING YOUR FLOW: DISCOVER YOUR PASSIONS AND ENGAGE IN ACTIVITIES THAT BRING YOU JOY AND FULFILLMENT.

In the tapestry of life, there exists a state of being that transcends the mundane and elevates our existence to a realm of pure joy and fulfillment. This state, often referred to as "flow," is a phenomenon characterized by complete immersion in an activity, a loss of self-consciousness, and a heightened sense of enjoyment. Finding your flow is a journey of self-discovery, a process of uncovering your passions and engaging in activities that ignite your soul and bring you a deep sense of satisfaction.

The concept of flow was first introduced by psychologist Mihaly Csikszentmihalyi, who described it as a state of optimal experience in which we are fully engaged in what we are doing, losing track of time and feeling a sense of effortless joy. Flow occurs when our skills are perfectly matched to the challenge at hand, creating a harmonious balance between our abilities and the demands of the task.

Discovering your passions is the first step towards finding your flow. What activities make you lose track of time? What do you love doing so much that you would do it for free? What are your natural talents and abilities? Exploring these questions can help you identify the activities that are most likely to bring you into a state of flow.

Passions are not just hobbies or interests; they are the driving forces behind our purpose and fulfillment. They are the things that make us feel alive, energized, and excited. When we engage in activities that we are passionate about, we tap into our innate creativity and potential. We become fully immersed in the present moment, losing ourselves in the joy of creation and expression.

Engaging in activities that bring us joy and fulfillment is not a luxury; it is a necessity. When we are happy and fulfilled, we are more productive, creative, and resilient. We are better able to cope with stress, overcome challenges, and maintain healthy relationships. Joy and fulfillment are the cornerstones of a meaningful life.

Finding your flow is not always easy. It requires a willingness to experiment, to try new things, and to step outside of your comfort zone. It also requires a commitment to self-awareness and self-reflection. By paying attention to how you feel when you are engaged in different activities, you can begin to identify the ones that bring you the most joy and fulfillment.

Once you have found your flow activities, it's important to make time for them regularly. Schedule them into your calendar, prioritize them, and protect them from distractions. The more you engage in activities that bring you into flow, the easier it will become to access this state of being.

Flow is not just about individual enjoyment; it also has a positive impact on the world around us. When we are in flow, we are more creative, productive, and innovative. We are more likely to make meaningful contributions to our communities and the world at large.

Finding your flow is a journey of self-discovery, a process of uncovering your passions and engaging in activities that ignite your soul and bring you a deep sense of joy and fulfillment. It is a journey that is worth taking, for it leads to a life that is rich, meaningful, and rewarding.

ᏆᏆᏆ

*Your obstacles are not roadblocks but stepping stones to your success. Develop resilience and perseverance, and navigate challenges with grace. Remember, every challenge you overcome makes you stronger and wiser.*

# ELEVEN

# OVERCOMING OBSTACLES: DEVELOP RESILIENCE AND PERSEVERANCE TO NAVIGATE CHALLENGES WITH GRACE.

Life is a journey filled with both triumphs and tribulations. The path to achieving our dreams is rarely smooth, often fraught with unexpected twists, turns, and obstacles. However, it is precisely in these challenges that we have the opportunity to grow, to learn, and to discover our true strength. Overcoming obstacles is not about avoiding them but about developing the resilience and perseverance to navigate them with grace.

Resilience is the ability to bounce back from adversity, to adapt to change, and to maintain a positive outlook even in the face of setbacks. It is the inner strength that allows us to persevere through difficult times, to learn from our mistakes, and to emerge stronger and wiser on the other side.

Resilience is not about being invincible; it is about being flexible, adaptable, and willing to embrace the challenges that life throws our way.

Perseverance, on the other hand, is the steadfastness in doing something despite difficulty or delay in achieving success. It is the unwavering determination to pursue our goals, no matter what obstacles we encounter. Perseverance is the fuel that keeps us going when the going gets tough, the inner fire that ignites our passion and propels us forward.

Developing resilience and perseverance is a lifelong journey, a process of continuous learning and growth. It begins with a mindset shift, a change in perspective from viewing obstacles as roadblocks to seeing them as opportunities for growth.

When we encounter a challenge, instead of giving up or feeling defeated, we can choose to see it as a chance to learn, to adapt, and to become stronger.

Cultivating a growth mindset is essential for developing resilience and perseverance. A growth mindset is the belief that our abilities and intelligence can be developed through dedication and hard work. It is the understanding that challenges are not a reflection of our worth or potential, but rather opportunities for learning and growth.

By embracing a growth mindset, we open ourselves up to the possibility of overcoming any obstacle and achieving our dreams.

Another key factor in developing resilience and perseverance is learning to manage our emotions effectively. When we encounter setbacks or failures, it is natural to feel discouraged, frustrated, or even angry. However, if we allow these negative emotions to consume us, they can paralyze us and prevent us from moving forward.

By learning to identify and manage our emotions, we can regain control of our thoughts and actions, and channel our energy towards finding solutions and overcoming challenges.

Building a strong support system is also crucial for developing resilience and perseverance. Surrounding ourselves with positive, supportive people who believe in us and our dreams can make all the difference when faced with adversity. They can offer encouragement, guidance, and a shoulder to lean on when we need it most.

A supportive community can also provide us with valuable resources and opportunities, helping us navigate challenges and achieve our goals.

In addition to these strategies, there are many other practices that can help us develop resilience and perseverance. These include mindfulness, meditation, yoga, exercise, and spending time in nature. These practices help us to cultivate inner peace, reduce stress, and connect with our inner strength and wisdom.

The journey of overcoming obstacles is not always easy, but it is always worthwhile. By developing resilience and perseverance, we equip ourselves with the tools we need to navigate life's challenges with grace and emerge stronger on the other side. We learn to embrace our failures as opportunities for growth, to persevere through difficult times, and to never give up on our dreams.

Remember, every obstacle we overcome makes us stronger, wiser, and more resilient. The journey is not about avoiding challenges, but about facing them head-on with courage, determination, and grace. By doing so, we not only achieve our goals but also discover our true potential and live a life of purpose and fulfillment.

ϷϷϷ

*Your imagination is a powerful tool for manifestation. Visualize your dreams in vivid detail, and feel the emotions of already having achieved them. Remember, what you can envision, you can create.*

# TWELVE

# The Art of Visualization: Use visualization techniques to bring your dreams to life in vivid detail.

Visualization, often hailed as a powerful tool for manifestation, is the art of creating a mental picture of your desired reality. It is the act of consciously using your imagination to bring your dreams to life in vivid detail, engaging all your senses to experience the sights, sounds, smells, tastes, and touch of your desired outcome. By harnessing the power of visualization, you can tap into the creative energy of the universe, aligning your thoughts, feelings, and actions with your goals and aspirations.

The principle behind visualization is rooted in the idea that our thoughts and emotions are energy, and that this energy interacts with the world around us. When we focus our minds on a specific outcome, we emit a vibrational frequency that attracts similar frequencies back to us. By visualizing our dreams as if they have already happened, we send a powerful message to the universe that this is what we desire and believe is possible. This unwavering faith and focused intention create a magnetic field that draws us closer to our goals.

Visualization is not just about daydreaming; it is a deliberate and intentional practice that requires focus, discipline, and consistency. To effectively visualize, it is essential to create a quiet space where you can relax and let go of distractions. Close your eyes, take a few deep breaths, and allow your mind to wander freely. Then, begin to envision your desired outcome as if it is happening in the present moment.

Engage all your senses in the visualization process. See yourself achieving your goal, hear the sounds of success, feel the emotions of joy and accomplishment, smell the fragrance of victory, and taste the sweetness of fulfillment. The more vivid and detailed your visualization, the more powerful it will be in imprinting your desired outcome on your subconscious mind.

Consistency is key to the success of visualization. The more often you visualize your dreams, the more deeply they become ingrained in your subconscious mind, and the more likely they are to manifest in your reality. Set aside a few minutes each day to visualize your desired outcome, whether it's in the morning upon waking or in the evening before bed.

As you practice visualization, pay attention to your emotions. The more positive and joyful you feel during your visualizations, the stronger the vibrational frequency you will emit, attracting more of those feelings into your life.

Visualization is not a magic wand that will instantly grant your wishes. It is a tool that can help you clarify your goals, focus your energy, and build your belief in your ability to achieve them. It is a powerful tool that can be used in conjunction with other manifestation techniques, such as setting intentions, taking action, and practicing gratitude.

The art of visualization is not just about achieving external goals; it is also about personal transformation. By visualizing ourselves as the person we want to become, we start to embody those qualities and characteristics. We become more confident, resilient, and empowered. We start to see ourselves as capable of achieving our dreams, and this belief fuels our actions and propels us towards our goals.

Incorporating visualization into your daily routine can have a profound impact on your life. It can help you overcome self-doubt, break through limiting beliefs, and tap into your full potential. It can improve your performance in various areas of your life, from sports and academics to relationships and career. Most importantly, it can help you manifest your deepest desires and create a life that is aligned with your values, passions, and purpose.

ppp

*Your intuition is your inner compass. Trust your gut instincts, and allow your inner wisdom to guide you on your path. Remember, your intuition knows the way; all you have to do is listen.*

# THIRTEEN

# CONNECTING WITH YOUR INTUITION: TRUST YOUR INNER WISDOM AND FOLLOW YOUR GUT INSTINCTS.

In the depths of our being lies a profound wellspring of wisdom, a silent guide that whispers truths beyond the realm of logic and reason. This inner knowing, often referred to as intuition, is a powerful compass that can navigate us through life's complexities, illuminating our path and leading us towards our highest good. Connecting with your intuition is a journey of self-discovery, a process of learning to trust your inner wisdom and follow your gut instincts.

Intuition is often described as a "gut feeling," a sense of knowing that arises from within, without the need for conscious reasoning or analysis. It is a subtle whisper that speaks to us through sensations, emotions, and subtle cues from our environment. Intuition is not a mystical power reserved for a select few, but a natural human faculty that we all possess. However, in a world that often prioritizes logic and reason, we may have learned to suppress or ignore our intuitive voice.

Connecting with our intuition requires us to quiet the noise of the external world and turn inward. It involves creating space for stillness, reflection, and self-awareness. Practices such as meditation, mindfulness, and spending time in nature can help us to tune into our inner wisdom and discern its subtle messages.

One of the most powerful ways to connect with your intuition is to simply pay attention to your body. Our bodies are incredibly intelligent and often communicate with us through physical sensations. A knot in your stomach, a tingling in your spine, or a sudden burst of energy may all be signs from your intuition. By learning to listen to these signals, we can gain valuable insights into our own needs, desires, and the best course of action.

Another key to connecting with your intuition is to trust your gut instincts. When faced with a decision or a challenge, take a moment to pause and check in with yourself. What does your gut tell you? What is your initial reaction? Often, our first instinct is the most accurate. By learning to trust our gut, we tap into a deep well of wisdom that can guide us towards the right choices.

Connecting with your intuition also involves recognizing and releasing any fears or doubts that may be blocking your inner knowing. Fear of the unknown, fear of failure, or fear of judgment can all cloud our intuition and prevent us from hearing its guidance. By identifying and addressing these fears, we can create space for our intuition to flourish.

Building trust in your intuition takes time and practice. Start by paying attention to the small intuitive nudges you receive in your daily life. Notice when your gut feeling leads you in the right direction, and acknowledge it. As you become more attuned to your intuition, you will gain confidence in its guidance and be more willing to follow it, even when it goes against conventional wisdom.

Trusting your intuition does not mean abandoning logic and reason. It is about integrating both your head and your heart, using both your intellect and your intuition to make informed decisions. Intuition can provide us with valuable insights and guidance, but it is important to weigh those insights against the available facts and information.

Connecting with your intuition is a journey of self-discovery, a process of learning to trust your inner wisdom and follow your gut instincts. It is a journey that can lead to greater self-awareness, empowerment, and fulfillment. By tapping into the power of your intuition, you can navigate life's challenges with grace and ease, make better decisions, and create a life that is aligned with your deepest values and aspirations.

ϸϸϸ

*Change is the only constant in life. Embrace the twists and turns of your journey with flexibility and openness. Remember, change is not an obstacle but an opportunity for growth and transformation.*

# FOURTEEN

## Embracing Change: Adapt to Life's Twists and Turns with Flexibility and Openness.

Life is an ever-flowing river, constantly shifting and changing its course. It is a dynamic dance of impermanence, where nothing remains the same. Embracing change is not merely a matter of survival but a pathway to growth, resilience, and ultimately, a more fulfilling life. It is about adapting to life's twists and turns with flexibility and openness, recognizing that change is not an obstacle but an opportunity for transformation.

Resistance to change is a natural human instinct. We crave stability, predictability, and control. We cling to the familiar, the comfortable, and the known. However, this resistance can become a source of suffering when we refuse to accept the inevitable truth that change is a constant in life. Whether it's a change in our personal circumstances, a shift in our relationships, or a global upheaval, change is a force that we cannot escape.

Embracing change requires a shift in mindset, a willingness to let go of the illusion of control and embrace the unknown. It is about accepting that life is a series of transitions, each one bringing new challenges and opportunities. By cultivating a mindset of flexibility and openness, we can navigate these transitions with grace and ease, allowing change to become a catalyst for growth and transformation.

Flexibility is the ability to adapt to new circumstances and situations. It is the willingness to bend without breaking, to adjust our course when necessary, and to find creative solutions to unexpected problems. When we are flexible, we are less likely to become overwhelmed or discouraged by change. We are able to see challenges as opportunities for learning and growth, and we are more likely to find joy and fulfillment in the journey.

Openness, on the other hand, is the willingness to consider new ideas, perspectives, and possibilities. It is the ability to step outside of our comfort zones and explore the unknown. When we are open, we are more receptive to change, more willing to embrace new experiences, and more likely to discover hidden talents and passions.

Embracing change is not about passively accepting whatever life throws our way. It is about actively engaging with change, seeking out opportunities for growth, and creating positive change in our own lives and the world around us. When we embrace change, we become co-creators of our own destiny, shaping our lives according to our values and aspirations.

There are many ways to cultivate flexibility and openness. One powerful practice is mindfulness, which involves paying attention to the present moment without judgment. By cultivating mindfulness, we become more aware of our thoughts, feelings, and bodily sensations, allowing us to respond to change with greater clarity and compassion.

Another helpful practice is to challenge our assumptions and beliefs. Often, our resistance to change stems from deeply ingrained beliefs about how things should be. By questioning these beliefs and considering alternative perspectives, we can open ourselves up to new possibilities and create space for change.

It is also important to develop coping mechanisms for dealing with the stress and uncertainty that often accompany change. These coping mechanisms might include exercise, meditation, journaling, or spending time in nature. By taking care of ourselves during times of transition, we can better navigate the challenges and emerge stronger on the other side.

Embracing change is a lifelong journey, a continuous process of learning and growth. It requires courage, resilience, and a willingness to let go of the familiar and embrace the unknown. By cultivating flexibility and openness, we can transform change from a source of fear and anxiety into a catalyst for growth, transformation, and ultimately, a more fulfilling life.

ppp

*Your sacred space is your sanctuary. Create a haven where you can recharge, reflect, and reconnect with your inner self. Remember, your sacred space is a portal to your inner peace and wisdom.*

# FIFTEEN

# CREATING A SACRED SPACE: DESIGN A SANCTUARY WHERE YOU CAN RECHARGE, REFLECT, AND RECONNECT WITH YOUR INNER SELF.

In our modern, fast-paced lives, filled with constant stimuli and demands, the need for a sanctuary, a sacred space where we can recharge, reflect, and reconnect with our inner selves, is more important than ever. This space, whether physical or metaphorical, serves as a haven from the external chaos, a place of solace where we can retreat to nurture our minds, bodies, and spirits. Creating such a space is a personal journey, a reflection of our individual needs, preferences, and values.

A sacred space is more than just a room or a location; it is an atmosphere, an energy, a feeling. It is a place where we feel safe, nurtured, and at peace. It is a place where we can let go of our worries, anxieties, and daily stresses, and simply be present in the moment. It is a place where we can connect with our inner wisdom, our intuition, and our higher selves.

The process of creating a sacred space begins with intention. It is a conscious decision to carve out a dedicated area in our lives for self-care, reflection, and spiritual nourishment. This space can be as simple as a cozy corner in your bedroom, a quiet spot in your garden, or a dedicated room in your home. The most important factor is that it feels safe, inviting, and conducive to relaxation and introspection.

Once you have chosen your space, it's time to personalize it. Fill it with objects that inspire you, uplift you, and bring you joy. This could include candles, crystals, plants, artwork, photographs, or any other items that hold special meaning for you. Consider adding elements that appeal to your senses, such as soft lighting, soothing music, or calming scents. The goal is to create an environment that nourishes your soul and promotes a sense of well-being.

Your sacred space can also be a place for spiritual practice. This could involve meditation, prayer, yoga, journaling, or any other activity that helps you connect with your inner self. By dedicating this space to your spiritual practice, you create a sacred container for your personal growth and transformation.

In addition to the physical space, creating a sacred space also involves establishing rituals and routines that support your self-care practice. This could include setting aside a specific time each day to spend in your sacred space, creating a ritual for entering and leaving the space, or simply taking a few deep breaths and setting an intention before beginning your practice.

The benefits of creating a sacred space are numerous and profound. It can help to reduce stress and anxiety, improve sleep quality, boost creativity, and foster a deeper connection with ourselves and the world around us. It can also serve as a reminder of our values, our dreams, and our purpose in life.

Creating a sacred space is not a one-time event but an ongoing process. It is a living, breathing entity that evolves and grows with us. As we change and grow, so too will our sacred space. It is important to revisit it regularly, to update it, refresh it, and infuse it with new energy.

In a world that is constantly pulling us in different directions, a sacred space offers a much-needed refuge, a place where we can slow down, recharge, and reconnect with our inner selves. It is a gift we give ourselves, a sanctuary where we can nurture our minds, bodies, and spirits. By creating a sacred space, we create a haven for our souls, a place where we can find peace, joy, and fulfillment.

ᐅᐅᐅ

*Your rituals are your anchors. Incorporate
meaningful practices into your daily life to enhance
your intentions and focus. Remember, rituals create
a sacred container for your energy and connect you
to the divine flow of life.*

# SIXTEEN

# THE POWER OF RITUAL: INCORPORATE RITUALS INTO YOUR DAILY LIFE TO ENHANCE YOUR INTENTIONS AND FOCUS.

Rituals, often associated with ancient traditions or religious practices, hold a potent power to transform our daily lives and enhance our intentions and focus. They are not merely symbolic gestures or empty routines, but rather intentional acts that create meaning, structure, and purpose in our lives. By incorporating rituals into our daily routine, we can tap into a deeper sense of connection, both with ourselves and the world around us.

At their core, rituals are a series of actions performed in a set order, often with a specific purpose or intention. They can be simple or elaborate, personal or communal, religious or secular. The key is that they are imbued with meaning and significance, creating a sense of sacredness and reverence. Rituals can be found in every culture and tradition, from morning prayers and meditation to tea ceremonies and coming-of-age rites.

The power of rituals lies in their ability to anchor us in the present moment, to focus our attention, and to create a sense of grounding and stability. By engaging in a ritual, we step out of the ordinary flow of time and enter a sacred space, where we can connect with our deeper selves and our intentions. Rituals create a container for our energy, allowing us to channel our focus towards a specific goal or outcome.

Incorporating rituals into our daily lives can have a profound impact on our well-being and productivity. They can help us to reduce stress, improve focus, enhance creativity, and cultivate a greater sense of purpose and meaning. Rituals can also serve as powerful reminders of our values and priorities, helping us to stay aligned with our goals and aspirations.

One of the most powerful ways to incorporate rituals into our daily lives is to create a morning routine. This could involve waking up at the same time each day, practicing meditation or yoga, journaling, or simply enjoying a cup of tea in silence. By starting our day with a ritual, we set the tone for the rest of the day, grounding ourselves in our intentions and priorities.

Similarly, creating a bedtime ritual can help us to wind down, relax, and prepare for a restful night's sleep. This could involve reading a book, taking a warm bath, or simply spending a few minutes reflecting on the day's events. By ending our day with a ritual, we signal to our bodies and minds that it is time to rest and recharge.

Rituals can also be used to mark significant life events, such as birthdays, anniversaries, or graduations. These rituals can help us to celebrate our achievements, honor our transitions, and connect with our loved ones. They can also serve as a reminder of our own mortality, inspiring us to live each day to the fullest.

Incorporating rituals into our work lives can also enhance our productivity and creativity. This could involve setting a specific time each day for deep work, taking regular breaks to move and stretch, or ending each day with a review of our accomplishments. By creating a structured and intentional work environment, we can optimize our focus and energy, leading to greater productivity and satisfaction.

The beauty of rituals is that they can be tailored to our individual needs and preferences. There is no right or wrong way to create a ritual. The most important thing is that it feels meaningful and authentic to you. Experiment with different rituals to see what resonates most deeply with you. As you incorporate rituals into your daily life, you will begin to experience their transformative power, enhancing your intentions, focus, and overall well-being.

ppp

*Your successes are your stepping stones. Acknowledge your achievements, big and small, and celebrate your progress. Remember, each victory is a testament to your strength, resilience, and unwavering spirit.*

# SEVENTEEN

# CELEBRATING YOUR SUCCESSES: ACKNOWLEDGE YOUR ACHIEVEMENTS, BIG AND SMALL, AND CELEBRATE YOUR PROGRESS.

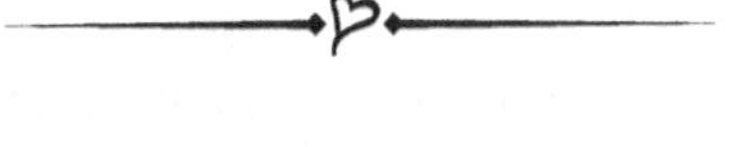

In the tapestry of life, woven with threads of dreams, aspirations, and efforts, successes are the vibrant hues that add color and vibrancy to our existence. Each achievement, big or small, is a testament to our dedication, perseverance, and growth. Celebrating these successes is not merely an act of indulgence but an essential practice that fuels our motivation, reinforces our self-belief, and propels us towards greater heights.

Acknowledging our achievements, both the monumental milestones and the seemingly insignificant steps forward, is a vital component of celebrating our progress. It is a recognition of the effort we have invested, the challenges we have overcome, and the lessons we have learned along the way.

By taking the time to pause and acknowledge our successes, we honor our journey and give ourselves permission to feel proud of what we have accomplished.

Celebrating our successes is not about vanity or self-aggrandizement; it is about cultivating a positive mindset and reinforcing our self-worth. When we celebrate our achievements, we send a powerful message to our subconscious mind that we are capable, worthy, and deserving of success.

This positive reinforcement strengthens our self-belief, boosting our confidence and empowering us to pursue even greater goals.

Furthermore, celebrating our successes is a way of expressing gratitude for the opportunities, resources, and support that have enabled us to achieve our goals. It is a recognition of the contributions of others, whether it be our mentors, colleagues, friends, or family.

By acknowledging and appreciating the help we have received, we cultivate a sense of gratitude and interconnectedness, strengthening our relationships and creating a positive ripple effect in the world.

The act of celebrating our successes can take many forms. It can be as simple as taking a moment to reflect on our achievements and express gratitude for them. It can involve sharing our successes with loved ones, receiving their congratulations and encouragement.

It can also be a more elaborate celebration, such as throwing a party, treating ourselves to a special experience, or simply taking a break to relax and recharge.

The key is to find ways to celebrate that resonate with you and that feel authentic and meaningful. It is important to acknowledge and celebrate not only the big wins but also the small victories along the way. Each step forward, no matter how small, is a reason to celebrate.

By acknowledging and appreciating our progress, we stay motivated, energized, and focused on our goals.

Celebrating our successes also serves as a powerful reminder of our resilience and strength. It reminds us that we have the ability to overcome challenges, to persevere through difficult times, and to emerge stronger on the other side. By acknowledging our past successes, we tap into our inner strength and resilience, empowering us to face future challenges with confidence and determination.

Moreover, celebrating our successes is a way of giving ourselves permission to experience joy and fulfillment. It is a reminder that life is not just about achieving goals but also about enjoying the journey. By celebrating our successes, we infuse our lives with joy, gratitude, and a sense of accomplishment.

We create a positive feedback loop that reinforces our motivation and inspires us to continue striving for our dreams.

In a world that often focuses on what we haven't yet achieved, celebrating our successes is a radical act of self-love and acceptance.

It is a declaration that we are enough, that we have enough, and that we are worthy of celebrating our accomplishments. By embracing this practice, we not only enhance our well-being and happiness but also inspire others to do the same.

Remember, celebrating your successes is not a sign of arrogance or egotism. It is a healthy and necessary practice that fuels your motivation, reinforces your self-belief, and propels you towards greater heights. So, take the time to acknowledge your achievements, big and small, and celebrate your progress. You deserve it!

ᐳᐳᐳ

*Your gifts are meant to be shared. Use your talents to make a positive impact on the world around you. Remember, your contributions, no matter how small, can create a ripple effect of kindness and compassion.*

# EIGHTEEN

# GIVING BACK TO THE WORLD: USE YOUR GIFTS AND TALENTS TO MAKE A POSITIVE IMPACT ON OTHERS.

In the intricate dance of life, each of us possesses unique gifts and talents, a treasure trove of potential waiting to be unleashed upon the world. These gifts, whether artistic, intellectual, emotional, or practical, are not meant to be hoarded or hidden, but to be shared and celebrated. Giving back to the world is not just an act of altruism; it is a profound expression of our humanity, a way to connect with others, create meaning, and leave a lasting legacy.

Our gifts and talents are not mere accidents of birth; they are a reflection of our unique essence, our divine spark. They are the tools through which we can express our creativity, passion, and purpose.

By using our gifts to make a positive impact on others, we tap into our full potential and contribute to the greater good. We become agents of change, creating ripples of kindness, compassion, and inspiration that touch the lives of countless others.

The act of giving back is not limited to grand gestures or heroic deeds. It can be as simple as offering a listening ear to a friend in need, volunteering our time at a local shelter, or sharing our knowledge and skills with others. The most important factor is that we are using our gifts and talents in a way that benefits others, that uplifts and empowers them.

The impact of giving back goes far beyond the recipients of our generosity. It also has a profound effect on ourselves. When we give to others, we experience a sense of joy, fulfillment, and purpose. We connect with our own humanity and recognize our interconnectedness with all beings. We develop a greater appreciation for our own gifts and talents, as we witness their transformative power in the lives of others.

Giving back also fosters a sense of gratitude. When we focus on the blessings in our lives and the opportunities we have to make a difference, we cultivate a grateful heart that attracts even more abundance into our lives. Gratitude is a powerful emotion that opens our hearts, expands our minds, and deepens our connection to the world around us.

The act of giving back is not a one-way street; it is a reciprocal exchange of energy and love. When we give to others, we receive in return. We receive the joy of making a difference, the satisfaction of contributing to something bigger than ourselves, and the gratitude and appreciation of those we have helped. This positive feedback loop reinforces our desire to give, creating a virtuous cycle of generosity and abundance.

Furthermore, giving back can be a powerful antidote to feelings of isolation and alienation. When we connect with others through acts of service, we build bridges of understanding, compassion, and empathy. We create a sense of community and belonging, reminding us that we are not alone in this journey called life.

The possibilities for giving back are limitless. We can use our artistic talents to create beauty and inspire others, our intellectual gifts to educate and empower, our emotional intelligence to heal and uplift, and our practical skills to build and create. The key is to find a way to use our gifts and talents in a way that aligns with our values and passions.

When we give back to the world, we leave a lasting legacy. Our actions, no matter how small, can have a ripple effect that extends far beyond our own lives. We can inspire others to give, to share their gifts, and to make a positive impact in their own communities. We can create a more compassionate, just, and equitable world, one act of kindness at a time.

Giving back to the world is a powerful way to express our gratitude, connect with others, and make a difference. It is a journey of self-discovery, a process of uncovering our gifts and talents and using them to create a better world. By embracing the spirit of giving, we not only enrich the lives of others but also our own, creating a life that is both meaningful and fulfilling.

ppp

*Your life is a tapestry of values, passions, and purpose. Live in alignment with your authentic self, and create a life that is a true reflection of your heart's desires. Remember, you are the artist of your own life; paint it with the colors of your soul.*

# NINETEEN

## Living in Alignment: Integrate Your Values, Passions, and Purpose into Your Everyday Life.

Living in alignment is a harmonious state of being, where our actions, choices, and values are in congruence with our deepest passions and purpose. It's a life lived with intention, authenticity, and integrity, where we feel a deep sense of fulfillment and joy. However, in the fast-paced, ever-changing world, it's easy to lose sight of our true selves and drift away from our core values. Integrating our values, passions, and purpose into our everyday lives is a continuous journey of self-discovery, reflection, and intentional action.

At the heart of living in alignment lies self-awareness. It's about understanding our core values, those fundamental beliefs that guide our decisions and actions. What is truly important to us? What principles do we hold dear? What kind of impact do we want to make in the world? Taking the time to reflect on these questions can help us gain clarity on our values and ensure that they are reflected in our daily lives.

Our passions are the fuel that ignites our souls, the activities that bring us joy, excitement, and a sense of purpose. They are the things we love doing, the things we lose ourselves in, the things that make us feel alive. Identifying our passions and incorporating them into our daily lives is a crucial step towards living in alignment. When we engage in activities that we are passionate about, we tap into our creative energy, unleash our full potential, and experience a deep sense of satisfaction and fulfillment.

Purpose is the overarching goal or mission that gives meaning to our lives. It's the reason we get up in the morning, the driving force behind our actions, the compass that guides our decisions. Discovering our purpose can be a lifelong journey, but it's a journey worth taking. When we live a life that is aligned with our purpose, we feel a sense of direction, focus, and meaning. We are motivated to make a difference in the world, to leave a lasting legacy.

Integrating our values, passions, and purpose into our everyday lives requires intentionality and commitment. It's about making choices that are aligned with our authentic selves, even when they are difficult or unpopular. It's about saying "no" to things that don't serve us and "yes" to opportunities that align with our values and passions. It's about creating routines and habits that support our well-being and our purpose.

Living in alignment also involves setting boundaries, both with ourselves and with others. It's about learning to say no when we need to, protecting our time and energy for the things that truly matter. It's about communicating our needs and expectations clearly and assertively, creating healthy relationships that support our growth and well-being.

It's important to remember that living in alignment is not a destination but a journey. It's a continuous process of learning, growing, and evolving. As we change and mature, our values, passions, and purpose may also shift. The key is to remain open to these changes, to embrace them as opportunities for growth, and to continue to make choices that are aligned with our authentic selves.

The benefits of living in alignment are numerous and profound. It can lead to greater happiness, fulfillment, and inner peace. It can enhance our creativity, productivity, and overall well-being. It can also lead to more meaningful and fulfilling relationships, as we attract people who share our values and passions.

Living in alignment is a choice, a decision we make every day to live a life that is true to ourselves. It is a journey of self-discovery, a process of uncovering our values, passions, and purpose, and integrating them into our everyday lives. By embracing this journey, we can create a life that is both joyful and meaningful, a life that is in alignment with our deepest desires and aspirations.

PPP

*Your journey of manifestation is an ongoing process of growth and evolution. Embrace the twists and turns, the challenges and triumphs, as you create the life of your dreams. Remember, you are a powerful creator, capable of manifesting a life that is beyond your wildest imagination.*

# TWENTY

# THE JOURNEY OF MANIFESTATION: EMBRACE THE ONGOING PROCESS OF GROWTH AND EVOLUTION AS YOU MANIFEST YOUR DREAMS.

The journey of manifestation is a profound and transformative path, one that invites us to embark on a continuous process of growth and evolution as we bring our dreams to fruition. It is not a destination but a dynamic and ever-unfolding adventure, filled with twists and turns, challenges and triumphs. Embracing this journey requires a shift in perspective, a willingness to let go of the illusion of control and embrace the uncertainty inherent in the creative process.

Manifestation, at its core, is the act of consciously co-creating our reality. It is the understanding that our thoughts, feelings, and beliefs have a profound impact on the world around us. By aligning our intentions with the universal flow of energy, we can attract our desires into our lives. However, manifestation is not a quick fix or a magic formula; it is a process that requires patience, perseverance, and a willingness to surrender to the wisdom of the universe.

The journey of manifestation begins with a seed of desire, a spark of inspiration that ignites our imagination and sets our hearts ablaze. This seed, once planted in the fertile soil of our consciousness, begins to germinate, taking root and growing into a vision of our desired reality. It is through this vision that we set our intentions, clarify our goals, and begin to take inspired action.

As we embark on this journey, we encounter various challenges and obstacles that test our resolve and resilience. We may face setbacks, disappointments, and moments of doubt. However, it is precisely in these challenges that we have the opportunity to grow and evolve. We learn valuable lessons about ourselves, our strengths, and our weaknesses. We discover hidden reserves of courage, creativity, and determination.

Embracing the ongoing process of growth and evolution is essential for manifesting our dreams. It is about recognizing that we are not static beings but dynamic, ever-changing entities. Our desires, beliefs, and goals may shift and evolve as we learn and grow. This is not a sign of failure but a natural part of the process. By remaining open to change and willing to adapt our course, we allow ourselves to flow with the current of life, rather than resist it.

The journey of manifestation is also a process of surrender. It is about letting go of the need to control every aspect of our lives and trusting in the wisdom of the universe. It is about surrendering to the flow of life, allowing it to guide us towards our highest good. This does not mean giving up on our dreams or becoming passive observers of our lives. Rather, it means recognizing that we are co-creators of our reality, working in partnership with the universe to manifest our desires.

As we surrender to the flow of life, we begin to notice synchronicities, coincidences, and unexpected opportunities that guide us towards our goals. We become more attuned to our intuition, our inner compass that points us in the right direction. We learn to trust the process, even when we cannot see the full picture.

The journey of manifestation is a transformative experience that goes far beyond the achievement of our goals. It is a journey of self-discovery, growth, and evolution. It is a journey that leads us to a deeper understanding of ourselves, our connection to the universe, and our role in the grand scheme of things. By embracing the ongoing process of growth and evolution, we open ourselves up to a life of limitless possibilities, a life filled with joy, abundance, and fulfillment.

ඬඬඬ

*Your dreams are your birthright. Step into your power, embrace your unique gifts, and create a life that radiates with joy, abundance, and fulfillment. Remember, you are a woman of infinite potential, and your dreams are waiting to be realized.*

# TWENTY-ONE
## SUMMARY

Embarking on the journey of manifesting dreams is a transformative endeavor that empowers women to create a life of intention, purpose, and fulfillment. It is a journey that calls upon our inner visionary, harnessing the power of intention, gratitude, and self-belief to manifest our deepest desires into reality.

The first step in this journey is to awaken our inner visionary, to uncover our deepest desires and create a compelling vision for our lives. This involves a deep dive into self-reflection, exploring our passions, values, and beliefs. By identifying what truly ignites our souls, we can craft a vision that serves as our North Star, guiding us towards our dreams and aspirations.

Once we have a clear vision, it is time to harness the power of intention. This involves setting clear goals, cultivating a strong belief in their possibility, and taking aligned action towards their realization. By focusing our thoughts, feelings, and actions on our desired outcomes, we create a magnetic field that attracts the resources, opportunities, and people necessary to manifest our dreams.

Gratitude plays a crucial role in the manifestation process. By embracing a grateful mindset, we open ourselves up to abundance in all areas of our lives. Gratitude is not just about saying thank you; it is a conscious choice to focus on the good in our lives, to appreciate the blessings, both big and small, that we often take for granted. This shift in perspective opens the door to a wealth of possibilities, allowing us to see and seize opportunities that we might otherwise miss.

Releasing limiting beliefs is another essential step in manifesting our dreams. These are the negative thought patterns and self-doubt that hold us back from reaching our full potential. By identifying and challenging these beliefs, we can break free from their grip and create a more empowering narrative for ourselves.

Designing our dream life involves crafting a roadmap for our ideal future, aligning our actions with our goals. It's about setting SMART goals, taking inspired action, and making choices that support our vision. It's about creating routines and habits that nurture our well-being and propel us towards our dreams.

The art of self-care is a non-negotiable aspect of manifesting our dreams. It involves nurturing our minds, bodies, and spirits through practices such as meditation, exercise, healthy eating, and spending time in nature. By taking care of ourselves, we create a strong foundation for success and fulfillment.

Embracing imperfection is another key principle in the journey of manifestation. It's about accepting our flaws and celebrating our unique journey of growth. By letting go of the need for perfection, we free ourselves from the burden of comparison and self-criticism, allowing us to show up as our authentic selves.

Positive affirmations are powerful tools for reprogramming our subconscious minds and cultivating a positive mindset. By repeating affirmations that align with our desires, we can rewire our thought patterns and attract our desired outcomes into our lives.

Building a supportive community is crucial for staying motivated and inspired on our journey. Surrounding ourselves with like-minded individuals who uplift and encourage us can make all the difference when faced with challenges or setbacks.

Finding our flow is about discovering our passions and engaging in activities that bring us joy and fulfillment. When we are in flow, we tap into our creative energy, lose track of time, and experience a deep sense of satisfaction.

Overcoming obstacles is an inevitable part of the manifestation journey. By developing resilience and perseverance, we can navigate challenges with grace and emerge stronger on the other side.

The art of visualization is a powerful tool for bringing our dreams to life. By creating a vivid mental picture of our desired reality, we can imprint it on our subconscious mind and attract it into our lives.

Connecting with our intuition involves trusting our inner wisdom and following our gut instincts. Our intuition is a powerful compass that can guide us towards our highest good.

Embracing change is essential for growth and evolution. By adapting to life's twists and turns with flexibility and openness, we can navigate challenges with grace and embrace new opportunities.

Creating a sacred space is about designing a sanctuary where we can recharge, reflect, and reconnect with our inner selves. This space, whether physical or metaphorical, serves as a haven from the external world and a source of spiritual nourishment.

Incorporating rituals into our daily lives can enhance our intentions and focus. Rituals provide structure, meaning, and purpose, helping us to stay aligned with our goals and values.

Celebrating our successes, big and small, is crucial for reinforcing our self-belief and staying motivated on our journey. By acknowledging our achievements, we create a positive feedback loop that attracts more success into our lives.

Giving back to the world is a profound expression of our humanity and a way to connect with others. By using our gifts and talents to make a positive impact, we create a ripple effect of kindness and compassion.

ϷϷϷ

# Citation And References

This book represents the culmination of extensive research and meticulous analysis, incorporating a diverse range of sources, including numerous books, scholarly studies, and personal experiences. Additionally, I have scoured various websites to gather relevant information and data essential for the compilation of this work. I have taken every precaution to ensure the accuracy of the information presented and have diligently cited all sources to acknowledge their contributions.

Despite these efforts, the possibility of inadvertent errors remains. I deeply value the insights of my readers and appreciate any feedback that can help identify and rectify such inaccuracies. I encourage you to bring any discrepancies to my attention.

Your feedback is not only welcome but crucial, as it will aid in correcting current editions and enhancing the content of future ones. I am committed to maintaining the highest standards of accuracy and reliability in my work and thank you for your support and understanding.

Additionally, I firmly uphold the principle of freedom of speech and expression as guaranteed under Article 19(1)(a) of the Constitution of India, and I respect the diverse viewpoints and expressions of all readers.

ᛠᛠᛠ

# Other Books Of The Author

1. Empowering Minds: A Journey into Women's Self-Discovery and Power
2. The Dynamics of Motivation: Catalyzing Thought into Action
3. Meditation and Mental Well Being: The Path to Inner Peace and Clarity
4. The Psychology of Child Education: Nurturing Future Generations
5. Ethical Enlightenment: A Modern Guide to Living with Integrity
6. Voices of Empowerment: Stories of Women Rising Against Odds
7. Social Psychology in Everyday Life: Understanding Human Connections
8. The Essence of Motivational Speaking: Inspiring Change in Others
9. Balancing Acts: Women, Work, and the Will to Lead
10. Guiding with Grace: Raising Children with Compassion and Awareness
11. The Power of Positive Aging: Embracing Life After Fifty
12. Building Resilient Communities: Social Work in Action
13. The Ethical Educator: Principles for Teaching and Learning
14. From Insight to Impact: Social Psychology for a Better World
15. The Ethics of Empathy: A Guide to Ethical Living
16. The Science of Empowering the Self: Navigating Life's Challenges with Psychological Wisdom
17. The Mindful Conscious Leader: Meditation Techniques for Modern Management
18. Pioneering Spirit: Women's Pathways to Leadership and Empowerment
19. Feeling to Healing: The Role of Emotional Intelligence in Child Development
20. Transformative Talks and Words of Inspiration: Insights into Motivational Oratory

21. Green Ethics: A Path to Sustainable Living
22. Spiritual Integrity: Navigating Life with Moral Compassion
23. Clean Living, Clean Society: The Ethics of Cleanliness
24. Patriotic Spirits: Building a Nation on Positive Attitudes
25. Innovative Integrity & Vibrant Visions: The Ethical and Entrepreneurial Spirit of Gujarat
26. Youthful Visions, Endless Possibilities: Inspiring Ethics and Motivation in Children
27. Living Your Legacy: How to Motivate Others by Living Your Values
28. Secret of Healing Conversations: Ethical Practices in Counselling and Therapy
29. Creative Kindness: Crafting a Life of Compassion and Creativity
30. The Power of Appreciation: How Gratitude Can Transform Your Relationships
31. Bhagavad-Gita: Messages
32. Science of Art: The New Frontier of Fashion Modernism
33. Vivekananda's Virtues: A Blueprint for Modern Living
34. Empower Her: Navigating the Path to Women's Entrepreneurship
35. The Boundless Classroom: Innovations in Global Education
36. The Language of Leadership: Communicating with Authenticity and Impact
37. The Warrior's Mantra: Deciphering the Hanuman Chalisa
38. Echoes of Empathy: Transformative Stories of Social Service
39. Artful Living: Cultivating Creativity in Your Daily Routine
40. Finding Your Why: Discovering Your Passions and Charting Your Course
41. The Role of Social Media in Shaping Self-Esteem and Interpersonal Relationships among Adolescents
42. Karma's Tapestry: Weaving a Life of Selfless Service
43. Altruistic Alchemy: Transforming Lives Through Giving
44. The Blueprint of Pro-Activeness and Productivity: Crafting Habits for Success
45. The Simplicity with Grounded Wisdom: Embracing Authenticity

Bhajan
101.  Pilgrimage of the Soul: Spiritual Journeys in India

ඌඌඌ

• 133 •

# Contact

Dr. Minakshi Bansal
Social Activist
Ahmedabad, Gujarat, Bharat
minakshiindiag20@yahoo.com

❥❥❥

|| LOKAHA SAMASTHAHA SUKHINO BHAVANTU ||

9 798889 446860